THE MEANING OF LIFE

in a Nutshell

**WHAT GOD
WANTS YOU
TO KNOW**

DAVID P CALABRO

◆ FriesenPress

Suite 300 - 990 Fort St
Victoria, BC, Canada, V8V 3K2
www.friesenpress.com

Copyright © 2015 by DavId P Calabro
First Edition — 2015

All rights reserved.
All illustrations are copyright David P Calabro.

No part of this publication may be reproduced in any form, or by any means, electronic or mechanical, including photocopying, recording, or any information browsing, storage, or retrieval system, without permission in writing from FriesenPress.

ISBN
978-1-4602-7786-7 (Hardcover)
978-1-4602-7787-4 (Paperback)

1. Religion, Spirituality

Distributed to the trade by The Ingram Book Company

Table of Contents

People of the World viii
About The Book 1
How I Know What I Know 3
Early Childhood 5
My Family 11
What God Wants You To Know 12
Relationships 15
Healing Father Bednarik 20
My Body Double/Twin Flame(Doppelganger) 25
Cheating Death 28
Money Is Hard To Get 34
Basketball(Another Test from God) 36
Fantasy Turns into Reality 39
People and Their Beliefs 42
Investigator 45
My Father Died In 2003 47
Drama 49
No Operation 51
Strange Things 53
Astral Travels 57
Indian Powwows 63
Native Americans 65

Walk-In Spirit	70
Seeing My Father and Mother in Spirit	72
Thursday May 14th, 2015	72
Community College	75
How to Move in Space, the Fourth Dimension Way	78
Fourth Dimension vs. Fifth	79
A World Reporter	81
Tuesday, September 25th, 2012	82
Past Lives	88
Healing On My Own	90
The Reiki Healers	92
Going Crazy	94
Sleep Cycles	96
Politics	99
Our Military	101
Races	103
Genders	105
The Bible	107
Terrorists	109
Technology	111
Health	113
Mythical Creatures	116
The Devil	118
Death(Not Really)	120
God and Drama	122
Heaven	125

Dealing With People on Earth Each Day 127
Our Pets 129
Variations of Vibrations 133
Inspirations and Motivations 141
Thank You 143
Closing 145
Things to remember 148
Autograph 159
About The Author 160

People of the World

To the people of the world: the DNA in our bodies is changing for future Earth. It is God's will and for the good of all mankind.

Be ready for the great Earth change around November/December 2015 or spring of 2016. You can already see the great change in weather, earthquakes, volcanoes erupting, and odd creatures appearing all over the world. Our sun is acting stranger than ever, and don't forget asteroids whizzing by the planet, and alien beings appearing more and more with spaceships, even in daylight in front of thousands of people.

Wow! If this is not a wake-up call, I don't know what else is. By the way the spaceships are part of God's good army.

About The Book

This book will tell you "the real meaning of life in a nutshell." Sometimes it will be confusing; not everyone will get it. This is because your soul did not live enough former lifetimes and you are still a young soul, or because you are not eating and drinking the most natural foods and drinks you can consume each day.

Doing this makes the cells in your body have healthy DNA, which in turn lights up and gives energy to your pituitary master gland. This is a pea-sized part of your brain that is sometimes called the third eye, this master gland that scientists are mystified about and know very little about. You can't see it or detect it, but your God's soul is in this master gland. But I'm here to tell you this master gland is your soul of God's essence and energy, which puts you in line with God and the universe. Yes, this has been confirmed to me numerous times. Anytime I mention God to the Atheists, I mean our creator to you.

How I Know What I Know

Every time I question something in life or want to figure something out, God, angels and spirit guides, Saint Michael, Saint Germain, Saint Gabrielle, and the other saints give me the answer by a static electrical chill and then a loving warmth afterward to confirm it.

They sometimes don't answer right away if it's a complex issue because they need permission first or because they need more time to think about the situation. The reason is they know all the many moves ahead of time for these answers because the answer involves many people at once, you see! Like a chain of events. When they confirm an answer, my left and right brain start having chills, like a stereo vibration—Left-Right Left-Right Left-Right—then it goes down to my neck, shoulders, torso, lower half, and then legs, ankles, and toes!

Right after comes the warmth. They cover you in love. I just know it and feel it! The warmth is like a complete confidence they give me to assure me they are with me to cheer me on in this life, so to speak.

Early Childhood

I am 56 years old and a retired investigator for medical legal firms. I retired at 50 because I was tired of the hectic corporate world. As a kid, I grew up well rounded in South Philadelphia, Delaware County, Folcroft, PA, and South West Philadelphia.

My mother and father always took me to Atlantic City, where my grandmother and grandfather had a small row home. Days in Atlantic City were good back then. There were NO CASINOS!

A day on the beach and some military army men toys or cowboys and Indian men kept me busy. Don't forget the little Matchbox cars and Hot Wheels.

At home in Folcroft, PA was nice. We had an end-of-row large yard to play in and went swimming, and in the winter made the best snowmen and snow angels! Camping out in our yard all night long was great for young kids, fun fun fun!!!

Growing up in my preteen years, I didn't know it at the time, but in my 50s, when I went to psychics, they said my Aunt Rita was a psychic and so was my grandmother. Also my father was slightly psychic and a healer. He could ease your mind with his voice and his aura could command that you listened or else!

My dad and I were close and went everywhere together. My brothers would get jealous of me. Dad was a World War II vet who fought in Japan. He would tell me stories of how he and the men would come off of the amphibious watercraft to land on the Japanese beaches. When they did, my dad would look around on the beach and see all of his men dead. Just he and a few others would survive. He told me he would constantly ask God, "Why did I survive?" I didn't know it at that time, but now that God the Creator made me smarter and gives me this knowledge, I know the reasons why.

My dad's promise to God, angels, and spirit guides in heaven before his soul was born out of the womb was: John J. Calabro, you wrote your life story and you promise to keep it. That you would raise a nice family with the good and not so good adventures in life, and you said you would have five children, but join the Marines first. Then would work at Curtis Publishing Co. in Philadelphia, followed by the Franklin Mint.

I went to the Mint, where they made anything out of gold, silver, and crystal. My dad even dipped my cross in gold from the many fine artists they have from around the world. We would have company picnics and barbeques, where I always entered the races and won! I could run like a deer!

Later in life it would come in handy for running the bases in baseball and being a running back in football. From ages 8 to 13 I held records for most touchdowns scored in the county. When we went to Longwood Gardens for the company, it was acres of well-manicured gardens, many acres of horticulture from round the world. The waterfalls were 25 feet tall with a huge koi pond. I loved feeding the koi fish. I said to my mom and dad, "I'm going to have those big fish some day!" I now have those koi fish.

My dad and I went everywhere together. Food shopping in South Philly to get all the best Italian foods every weekend for all the parties. We went to bars together and had roast beef sandwiches and shrimp in baskets.

When my grandmothers and aunts started dying, I was confused. I asked Mom and Dad, where does everybody go when you die? The answer was always in the ground and that's it. Boy that didn't seem too good. When I grew older and asked a priest, all they said was that we go to heaven, but they never explained anything else or elaborated on the subject. They always said, I want you to go home and say five *Hail Mary* and five *Our Father* prayers and everything will be all right. Yeah right, that didn't help me much at all.

Everywhere my dad and I went, and at any age growing up, he would say to me, "Are you really my son? You don't look it."

But why would he say that to me?

I'd say, "Of course I'm your son, Dad."

Dad would say, "I'm not sure. There's something odd about you. You're the black sheep of the family."

Throughout my childhood and teen years I was always a very good athlete at any sport. I was always on the starting team. It was a lot of fun winning championships and dating the cheerleaders! All American boy, huh. I even ran track at the University of Penn relays in the stadium. I went to Sharon Hill High School in the late 1970s, and graduated in 1977. My years there were cool, mostly having fun and goofing off. In school, I was a good artist besides athletics. I also liked history and map making.

I was an average C+ B student. A few of my classmates died of various circumstances and it was always the same routine. Boring: go to church, viewing home, to the grave. Nobody wondered and asked questions like me. This was the investigator coming out in me.

I didn't play high school football because you had six or seven guys ahead of you to play first. I didn't like that because I was used to being the starter. After my senior year, a couple of my friends said, "Dave, why don't you try out for semi-pro football?"

I thought about it for a while and then tried out.

The coaches saw that I was fast, tough, and smart for the game, so I started all four years. I switched to defensive back because I was tired of being tackled all the time as a running back. It made sense to me to give the pain and hit them, instead of taking the pain!

Those four years were some great ones. I met guys from other teams that were excellent players, all on my team. We had guys that were stars on college teams, guys from high school, and guys that went on to NFL and Canadian teams.

We were the Marcus Hook Oilers from the Sun Oil Company. We were good every year and played teams from Washington DC, New York, Philadelphia, Harrisburg, Delaware, New Jersey, Bucks County, and others. Great stuff!

I played 1979, 1980, 1981, 1982 and I had professional football tryouts for those years. Wow, what a ride! I partied with all the rock gangs, the disco gangs, and the sports gangs. Parties everywhere. Concerts everywhere. It was great! I played softball and football for Country Maid Deli in Delaware County, for Hasting Bar in Southwest Philly, and for South Philly Grille in South Philly. Every Wednesday, Thursday, Friday, Saturday, Girls Girls Girls everywhere. Life was great!

Then I met my wife, Irene, from South Philly.

After many girls I dated, God said, this is the one. My wife and I planned it from the other side in Heaven with the kids I'm told, 100% sure!

She said to me, "You're not traveling from city to city having girlfriends everywhere, if you want to be with me and raise a family. Besides do you want to get all broken up playing football?"

She had a point. So I chose the family life, with three kids, dogs, cats, birds, fish, and turtles. Wow!

My Family

My oldest son, David, is 29 and the first of our family to graduate with a Bachelor's degree in computer science. My daughter, Sabrina, is 24 and was the second to graduate, on her way to working in the medical field. My son Brandon is 22 and is a manager of major accounts for a local storage company. My wife, Irene, is an administrator in one of the country's largest defense contractors. They are manufacturers of commercial aircraft jets and have another division for space craft. Boy would I like to see those!

We still had good times, going to barbecues with friends and going to the beach on the east coast to Wildwood, NJ. We call it down the shore! We went to all the lakes fishing and having fun. So many funerals we went to and still nobody had the right answers!

What God Wants You To Know

God, angels, and guides would like all of mankind to know that we are made in their image. That doesn't mean looking like two eyes, a nose, ears, two arms and two legs. God means your soul. That special essence of energy light that is part of God, like himself. Yes, when we are up there in the realms we can do anything, and I mean anything that is not hurtful or damaging to any entity or thing. We are so happy that there is no reason to be negative at all.

He wants us to know that we are like superman and superwoman up there. We can levitate, appear and disappear, travel by flying ourselves or beam ourselves instantly from one place to another and it doesn't matter how far of a distance it is!

Here is another amazing thing we can do. We can actually split our heavenly bodies to project ourselves at least 2 or 3 times at the same time in different locations around our galaxy and the Universe! Yes I know it is hard to believe but it is 100% true! How wonderful is God now. Just like now we on Earth are a fleshy molecule projection of our real god-like selves up there. That's why people on Earth talk about body doubles or doppelgangers and study this on Earth. Fascinating. Hard to believe but sooo True!

This is how and why we are god-like. Also, since we are made of God's light we travel at the speed of light anywhere. When I astral travel I always see my relatives especially mom and dad looking different all the time. Whether they are 18-19 years old, or 40 years old, or 80 years old when I last saw them on Earth. They also change their clothes in an instant like the show Bewitched or a magic show. Isn't that great!

You'll never get a disease or get hungry or have to use the rest room ever, unless you want to envision it, then you can. You also will never get tired so you never need to sleep but you can simulate sleep if you want to. You can drive a vehicle if you want or fly or beam yourself on your own. You don't need a license for anything. You can't get hurt or crash. Even if you purposely run into each other your light bodies and vehicles will just go through each other. You can fly like an eagle off any high cliff and fly just like them. You can even project yourself to look like an eagle or anything. They don't call it paradise for nothing. You can be by yourself or with as many people or any animals you wish as long as you want to.

Sex on the other side is great because you read each others' minds but I won't tell you the rest. I'll just let you experience that yourself someday.

You can even travel to another planet in any galaxy to help or observe something. It's like watching a movie but you can actually do something in the movie without getting hurt. Great isn't it?

Or, you can write another life time of your life for your next storybook life of yourself because that's what each of us do up there all the time. Human beings by nature love drama and to observe and experience anything. That's who we are. We love to laugh and cry at times but try to laugh a little more while you're here. It's more fun anyway.

Remember, God wants you to know with all of these lifetime experiences you have, you will always be you and never ever cease to exist! Ever for eternity, so you can relax and smile again. God is great.

Relationships

I have been married for 33 years, wow! I can't believe Irene and I have gone this far. Eighty-five percent of all my friends have divorced. All the couples that divorce don't get the clues from God and the spirit world, and they just don't have common sense!

We have had many disagreements and some nasty arguing, but we always somehow worked it out. God always reminds you not to do what other couples do. So you learn from that. Oh, did your sister in law really break the windows of his car? Or did he scratch your car up or punch the wall in your living room, leaving a huge hole?

The results are being arrested, and having to put your own money out for the car because your insurance won't pay under the deductible. The hole you put in the wall you have to repair with your own hard-earned money, plus you broke or badly sprained your hand punching it. But that's the macho way and tough, hard core way, isn't it? Wrong way to go!

The first thing I do is try to iron it out verbally, but if that doesn't work, I just walk the dog to cool off and think how to repair what just happened. Do not use revenge! It will stress you out and it will only get worse.

Another way is to go to the mall by yourself or with a friend to get your mind off of things and to cool off, because right now you and your spouse are both hot. Ask your spirit guides to how to repair your relationship. Don't ask friends to help use revenge on your spouse. Remember, every revengeful action you do works against you in the other dimensions! Any repairing apology or nice thing you do is a plus up there. Always remember your spouse's spirit guides are watching you and talking it over with your guides!

Another way is to make a man cave in your basement or another room. Even make an addition to your house or patio enclosure. It should be somewhere you can always go, where nobody else can bother you, to relax and think about things.

You never solve anything by being stressed or when tensions are high. Relax in your man cave, with your spouse in another room, separated.

Remember to make your man cave a sanctuary, with everything that makes you happy! Start off with a big screen TV, then a refrigerator, and a comfy couple of chairs or couch with recliners. Add favorite photos and artwork of sports favorites, or you can have a movie theme! Bring one of your pets there with you. You can have a nice fish tank with cool fish. That would be your water therapy, with a wall of bubbles. Anything to relax and make your mind right!

On your big screen, you can put on your favorite funny shows or movies to make you laugh, or a sexy movie to remind you of your spouse for when you two make up. The crazier ideas, the better; be creative. I did for 33 years. God, angels, and guides are all about nice families, so they definitely want to see you back together. They're all watching you to see what kind of ideas you can come up with to make things better to make you think correctly. Get it? Got it!

The number one worst thing you can do is call the police and a lawyer! The police will give you a record and you certainly don't want that, and lawyers will 100% take most of your money and hers too! So none of you come out good.

Even if you do get money, and it's usually the woman who does, she won't get much, but she will blow the money on a 50- or 60-thousand-dollar car, when she should have bought one for 15 or 20 thousand. Then she will blow the money on other things and she'll wind up with no money left and miserable. She'll also be wishing to get back with you. It happens a lot. But you just blew the money on lawyers mostly. Leave them out!

If you never get back together again, she was just too greedy for the money and it was a mistake, so that one was not the one for you. God's timing will give you the right one, but money and greed are usually the culprits 90% of the time.

The monthly time for a woman is of course tricky, but God created this for us because all relationships need a time out. So the best thing for a guy is to go occupy himself with other interests. Stay busy and by the time 'it' is done, your wife will let you know when she is ready to get together. Don't fight because of this time out period, although your wife may want to take it out on you. You can just give her a hug and wait it out. But go do what you want to do and time will go by quicker, then she will come around to be her own self again.

Another thing to understand is that she might have an ailment that's bothering her or a problem with a relative, so understanding these things help a lot. In some circumstances there are women who fight and argue with us because they want to have sex. This is just how certain women are and there is nothing you can do about it. So either have sex or, if you can't take the way she is, then leave!

There is another time in a woman's life where they will just argue with you all the time. This is worse than your typical monthly time. It happens at about 45 to 55 years into a woman's life; men should stay away as much as possible. This is called "the big change." Whatever you say or do is always irritating to a woman, even though you're probably right.

God made this time in a woman's life so both partners can reflect and think hard and spiritually about their lives. This is a huge test in life and God's big test. At this time, it's okay to try a new hobby or travel with friends or join a new organization that you normally would not. You are re-exploring your life, in God's eyes, to learn more about everything in life!

Universal spirituality is the biggest thing you will experience, even exploring options from your religion to be one with God or the creator because they miraculously made you! This is the time to be one with the creator, to try to understand his/her meanings and messages in your life. You must question and wonder about everything, and ask the creator for you to be in tune with him/her and the other dimensions and universe. You will eventually get the answers!

Young and old, rich and poor, you will get to know the creator at some time, 100% definitely. So be patient, time works on the creator's time, not yours! The only thing wrong with this world is our government's greed for money! There is no money in the other dimensions. Get it? Got it!

Healing Father Bednarik

On one Sunday morning I was taking my son to work. It was about 9am. We walked to the truck and just as I opened the door, I noticed a purple ribbon cloth with gold stitched crosses on it. It was on the ground, so I picked it up. It was dirty but not worn. I called my wife and I told here about the ribbon. We both thought it was strange. I rolled it up in my right jacket pocket, and I said "when I get home, I would like you to wash it."

A lot of strange things happened to me and continue to happen to me. I get that feeling that tells me there is something more to this. I continued to drive my son to work, and then I dropped him off and started to drive home, when something hit me. As I thought about the holy ribbon, I put my right hand in my jacket pocket. I thought right away that this belongs to an altar boy, so I went to Saint Nicks church so I could find out who it belongs to and what kind of holy ribbon it is, and what it means.

This ribbon was a reminder to go to church. Three days ago I was walking down Broad street, and I saw a priest standing at the bus stop in front of the Methodist Hospital. I said to Father, "Nice day isn't it." Father Jim was what everyone called him and he said to me "yes it is but the bus is taking so long and I have to get back to Saint Nicks church." I said "I will give you a ride father, no problem." He was so happy. I said "my SUV is right there, let's go!"

As we were in the vehicle he expressed his thanks and I introduced myself. Then had told him I was writing a book about God, angels, and spirit guides. Father said "oh wow! Outstanding. I never met an author. Especially one in our neighborhood and writing a spiritual book at that."

I proceeded to drive him to Saint Nicks. When we arrived I gave him my card and asked Father Jim if he would pray for my book to be very successful. He said "no problem, I will pray for the book." When I dropped him off I said to myself I want to go to this church to see Father Jim at church when he is doing the mass. After the days passed I forgot, but you see the ribbon reminded me to go to church that day. When I arrived at the church, Father Jim was doing the mass.

The mass was 45 minutes long, and I was looking for father John Calabro because he has the same last name as me. I was sitting in the back at the last pew in the church, and I asked a woman if Father John Calabro belongs to this church. A woman told me he does. I wanted to speak with him. She said "No, Father John is at the The Annunciation church three blocks away on 10th street."

There was only 15 minutes left for the mass to end but I had to leave if I were to catch him at the other church. I arrived at the Annunciation church and walked down the aisle but the mass has just ended. Everyone was leaving so I saw Father up at the altar and I went up to him and asked, "Are you John Calabro?" The father said "no, I am Father Bednarik. Father John is out of town but I'm filling in for him."

We walked down the aisle together and spoke about my book and I also asked him to pray for my book. He replied yes I will pray for your book David. But you must pray for me. I asked why father and he said he had a nasty cold he could not get rid of for 2 week now.

As we were walking out of the church doors I shook his hand and held it a while. I could feel the heaviness in his energy. I immediately took out the purple ribbon with the gold crosses perfectly stitched out of my pocket and asked him, "Father, does this belong to one of the altar boys?"

He was so surprised and said "No! This is a healing ribbon for a priest! Where did you get this?"

I explained that I found it on the ground next to my SUV. I said that I was going to wash it at home, but he rolled it up and said that he needed the healing now for his nasty cold. He put it in his pocket and kept walking down the outside front steps of the church and said nothing else. I said but father I have to wash it for you. He just kept walking. Three days later I went to go see Father Bednarik. He told me that he was completely cured of that nasty cold and congestion. I asked him what day did you feel completely cured since I used to be an investigator? He said Monday the following day. I presented the healing ribbon the day before Sunday November 8th 2015. That Sunday night, I woke up at 3am to feel my lungs very heavy. I could hardly breathe. Being that I am an empath healer, this is what I was feeling, Father Bednarik's lungs cloud. This is what an empath healer is. Was it the holy healing ribbon? Was it me being an empath healer? Or was it a combination of both and a healing from above?

It certainly was not a coincidence.

So in conclusion, there are no coincidences. I was meant to drive Father Jim, to find that healing ribbon to remind me to go to church, to ask the lady about Father John, to go to the other church, to find Father Bednarik instead of Father John Calabro, to present Father Bednarik the holy healing ribbon with my empathic energy healing to heal Father Bednarik.

All coincidental? I think not!

Every persons lives are recorded before we are born. That's why God, angels, and guides know everything about us ahead of time. When we go to a psychic they are the ones speaking to the psychic to give us the information!

It feels great knowing that I helped heal a priest!

My Body Double/Twin Flame
(Doppelganger)

I first saw my body double in an astral travel in another dimension. My soul vibrated out of my body as usual and I said, "Okay where are you taking me this time?" I moved through the stars and I found myself going through the room of some building. It was dark, but like a movie theater. I heard fast-beat music and started to see flashing lights! I saw a few people starting to dance. I was sitting on one of the lounge couches. This was a nightclub! I said, "Oh cool!"

The music was great and the club was nice, clean and classy. I suddenly felt someone sitting next to me because I could feel their energy presence. I had to turn my head to the right slightly to be cautious and I thought I was looking in a mirror! It wasn't a mirror, because when I turned my head, my twin was looking at the dance floor!

He then turned his head toward me, facing me. WE were face to face for the first time! I thought I was looking in the mirror again, but it couldn't be. I put my hand up to his face and he just smiled! Wow! He didn't say anything at all, but he didn't have to. He just wanted to give me the message that he is real, my body double twin flame doppelganger! Everybody has one, but your soul has to be in tune with them. Read a book on them or think of them often.

I smiled and was shocked, floored, happy, and anything else you want to describe the great feeling. I enjoyed the music and the people dancing. Then suddenly I was being pulled back by my spirit guides. They know when it's enough to show you!

The second time I saw him was again in a movie theater type of place, but I was sitting in a director's chair high up, and I looked around and saw a strange runway. My twin body double came out of the back office area and sat next to me.

He looked the same as last time, like me! When he sat down he looked forward and I assumed I had to also. Then I heard music. An upbeat jam that made me dance in my chair. Then all of these models came on the runway to show their designer outfits. Some were women and some were guys. Nobody else was in the audience though, just me and my body double. I wondered why, but then he told me; mind telepathy of course. It was a rehearsal designer show benefit for that night. But again my spirit guides lifted me up and made me leave.

The third time was again in a movie theater type of place, but a big audience was there. The curtains opened up and the music started, but it was a Broadway play. This time my body double was not around so I watched the play and I couldn't believe it. He was the star of the play! The actors were all dressed differently in modern day street clothes like in New York City. They were all dancing to the beat and the crowd went wild. I was shocked and enjoyed the show, but I could only stay for the opening. Again, my spirit guides pulled me back and I went back to my body.

You can only stay a very short time each time because they just want to give you the message. That's all they are allowed to do, by God's terms. So my body double is a club owner, model, and actor!

Cheating Death

I've had many close calls, but I will just mention a few. One time I was playing football and blocking in the backfield as a running back when the ball was hiked. The ball was in play and this guy from the other team came straight for me, I blocked him, but he did something unusual that guys don't normally do. He came up under my chinstrap of my helmet and hit me with two of his fists at the same time in my throat. I could not breathe. He ruptured my Adam's apple so bad I had a lump in my throat for a year, and to this day I still have trouble swallowing. But I could have been a goner. I wasn't able to breathe, my angels were with me that day. Anyway, the play went for a big gain and we won the game.

Many years, at different times, I always looked up at the trees. I don't really know, why but trees fall! Do you know how many people get killed each year by trees? Either by a tree crashing through their house or on a car? Or this one... I was walking on a clear sunny day, no wind, on a sidewalk at the University of Pennsylvania. I was delivering filed documents for the hospital. In my mind, someone said, "Go across the street, Dave, and go see the football stadium you used to practice in." I took one step off the sidewalk into the street to cross, and a tree fell and crashed across the sidewalk. About 30 feet worth of crushing tree hit the sidewalk. A lot of people were around and saw it, but nobody was hurt. You see what I mean? No wind at all, sunny clear day, no apparent cause for this huge tree to come crashing down. I could have been a goner again.

Another time I was at a light in my car on Presidential Blvd in Bala Cynwyd, PA. In my rear view mirror, I saw a trash truck come over the hill behind me, speeding, I froze and didn't know where to move. I had to go! I was stuck. I said to myself, "This is it. He's not stopping."

He was blowing his horn and I thought I was a goner! The trash truck just missed me and it went through the red light and across City Avenue, a major busy street, clear to the other side up a hill like nothing ever happened and luckily it didn't hit any cars or anybody crossing. I just sat there at the light in shock and said my angels must be with me.

This next time there was a storm with hurricane winds and I was traveling for work to a law firm on a small road in a rural wooded area. It was a twisting road and the rain was coming down in sheets, but it was stranger because there was no rain a few seconds ago! While driving, I started to see mud slides from the creek bed and all of a sudden a huge tree about 50 feet tall fell across the road in front of me. I stopped in time and a couple of cars came up behind me to see if I was all right. Another close call. Chills again came to my head like stereo and I knew someone was with me!

There was a time I went into a bar where I sold my sports collectibles to all the guys. When I entered this bar, I couldn't see too well. It was filled with cigarette and cigar smoke, but a guy way across the other side of bar said, "There's that -bleep- -bleep- -bleep- -bleep- -bleep- -bleep-"

I never did any wrong or hurt anybody, but he walked around the bar with this handgun and said, "I oughta shoot you!" He tripped over another guy's foot and the gun went off, just missing me, and went right into the wood on the wall. I found out later from him that he was only kidding around and that he misses my coming into that bar with all of my sports collectibles. He's a huge Pittsburgh Steelers fan. The owner and bartender said to me, "He rarely gets like that, but Dave, he was actually joking around and it accidentally went off."

I saw him after that again at the bar the following week and that time he gave me a hug and said he was sorry, but said, "Where's my Pittsburgh Steelers stuff, man!" He was a good guy who often goes hunting in upstart Pennsylvania, so he's normally a good shot, but not this time. HA! Angels were there again.

There was a time around 9 p.m. at night, it had just turned dark and an electrical storm hit. While I was trying to get to the bar for the Eagles/Steelers game, the rain came down in sheets. While driving down Oregon Avenue, the street lights were knocked out for the entire area from the electrical storm, and gullies of water were streaming on the sidewalks. I drove along the road, under the train track overpass, where a large dip in the road shook the car. When the car came out, I was right on top of the intersection and hit an SUV. There were two young girls, 22 and 23 years old. When I hit, my arm crashed into the windshield, my head hit my arm, and all the airbags exploded and sent smoke everywhere. I looked around and said to myself (so I thought I was talking to myself), "What just happened?" I had never been in a car accident especially like this one. It seemed at the exact moment that it happened, I was moving in slow motion. Some people who have experienced an accident like this know what I mean.

I looked at my whole body to examine it and said, "What just happened? I'm really in a car crash." I looked at my right forearm and only had a 6-inch burn mark from the airbags, and shotgun blast burns from the powder. I asked, "How many angels do I have with me, five!?" And then the bells and whistles went off in my body. I really mean chills in my left side of my brain, then the right side, back and forth they went like stereo. Then down my neck, then both of my shoulders and continued to my torso. At that time, my head stopped the chills and started to get warm, warmth you've never felt, but there's something else in that warmth. There's a loving feeling you get with the warmth. You will never know unless you experience it. Then the chills (not like eating a water ice), not that kind of chill (brain freeze).

The chill traveled to my lower torso to my private areas and down my thighs and so on to my calves, feet, and toes! This was all followed by the loving warmth. Now that's love from God (the creator, for Atheists) and his army of angels and spirit guides. So I got out of the Lincoln Town Car, a heavy car, you know. The whole front of the car was smashed like an accordion, totaled!

The police and everyone came so fast, even in this electrical storm. The girls were all right because they were in the front and I hit the side rear of their SUV. The girls said to me and the police that they didn't want to ride through the stream of water—about two feet high near the curb—because they didn't want to get stuck, so they didn't know what to do being so young of drivers, but I forgave them. They just stayed in the middle of the intersection in the dark.

I have more and more stories to tell of near death experiences and close calls, but there's too many to mention. The good stuff comes later in this book.

I've been examined time and time again by top doctors at Jefferson University and the Rothman Institute and there is nothing wrong with me. I eat all natural foods and drinks. I don't go to bars anymore, except once in a while on a Friday night to relax and counsel people. I exercise in the park, which locals call 'the lakes,' and which is nearby where the Philadelphia Eagles practice and play. I say my sincere prayers every day and night. God and the angels always like it when I thank them and compliment them!

Money Is Hard To Get

At one time I worked three jobs at once because I really wanted this car, but I was so tired working for it I came close to killing myself two times before I said, "That's it." I quit two jobs and kept the one. I crossed over into opposing lanes of traffic on MacDade Boulevard a couple of times, after working the 12 a.m. to 8 a.m. shift. So much for making money.

Over the course of two years, I played the PA lottery, three different games: Megaball, Cash 5, Treasure Hunt. All 29 times I missed the jackpot by <u>ONE NUMBER</u>. Amazing! I am still astonished today! I never knew the reason until now. They tell me that I must stay poor to learn all walks of life, everywhere I go! Besides all people, I must learn all animals, insects, and plants to know the true meaning of life, including wars and politics.

The Meaning of Life in A Nutshell

So that's why they didn't want me to have money in that form. They tell me in the near future I will have big money. But, when I do get it, I'm still basically going to do the same things I'm doing now and just feel good about having big money. God won't let me have it yet because I am on a special mission from the creator (God)!

Everyone on my street block is just about a millionaire, plus their houses are paid off. One guy has a mansion on the block and this is a row-home street with Italian-style balconies. He also bought up one quarter of the homes on my street. We have attorneys, stock brokers, MRI technicians, computer engineers, nurses, mechanics for hospitals, hunters that own game lands upstate, and old ladies with huge inheritances! I am the poorest on the blocks with $0 in my bank account. I asked every one of them for a small donation to write this book and they all refused with different excuses! And I know these neighbors very well and we talk all the time, but they're greedy and money hungry. They won't even part with a little to help a good neighbor. I helped all of them from time to time with errands, fixing flat tires, helping them in the winter snow. I even give them spiritual advice, counseling to them for free, no charge! God does not want me to charge anybody for life's knowledge. God is keeping me poor until I get this book out to the world so people may know the true "meaning of life in a nutshell."

Basketball
(Another Test from God)

When I was growing up, I was a good point guard in basketball. When I started working at MCS in Philadelphia, I worked with two African American guys who were bragging about how good their basketball teams were. One guy was from North Philly, and the other was from West Philly, Will Smith's old stomping grounds!

I jumped in the conversation and they both came down on me hard. Saying things like, "You don't know anything about basketball, old man." They laughed and said, "We will tell you when the next league starts up and you can play in the league with your team." And they started laughing every day I saw them. Now me, being shy growing up, I thought, I can never get a team to beat those guys!

So I thought.

I said to myself, "I can never do it. I'm scared, I'm going to embarrass myself."

"God works in mysterious ways"

Any time I mention God in this book, I mean God's army of twelve different angels and spirit guides, plus all of the souls that died.

But with God on my side, I prayed and started going to basketball playgrounds, looking for the best players. I could have recruited the guys I just know, but they weren't that good, but they were pretty good. To beat those teams, I had to have a super team from God that would win championships. Plus, I didn't know how to speak to these giants, let alone convince them to play for my team. Remember this is called the Unlimited League. Just before the NBA, it contains the best college and playground players in the city. Biggest and the best in Philadelphia.

I saw a couple of guys in an all-black neighborhood play and I talked to people on the sidelines. They said those two guys play well together, meaning the two guards. They know each other's moves, even if they are not looking. They have been playing together since they were little kids. Somehow God gave me enough confidence to ask them after the game and I was shocked they wanted to play on my team. All I said was:

"I'm going to put together a super all-star team from God."

That's all it took!

Then I started to travel outside the neighborhood and recruited players that played at top colleges. I also recruited a seven-foot-two-inch guy from the European League who lived across the bridge in Cinnaminson, New Jersey. Now I had a team. Rebounders, point guards, three point shooters. One of the guys told me about the Philadelphia 76ers tryout camp on City Line Ave. at the PECOM gym building.

So I managed to get two players that could not make the 76ers team. We played in five straight leagues and won five straight championships! Wow, until this day I have the trophies down in my man cave.

To recap on the moral of the story, God and God's Army still work in mysterious ways and always will! Here I was, an older guy, still shy, who couldn't recruit or afraid to ask people to join the team, and I did under God's power. He also made me travel to different areas I normally would not dare go, like the badlands and the hood, but I did. I went to places that were scary in the daytime and where I was the only white person around! He gave me the confidence to talk to strangers and told me exactly what to say perfectly and the timing was perfect too!

What started as a bet between two guys and myself was a life lesson. I won the championships and gained the respect from the two guys, plus they wanted to play for me! I said, "Sorry fellas, you know my guys are better players."

Fantasy Turns into Reality

Let's take a closer look at this and think. All I know is up there. They tell me that fantasy—almost every time, if not now, then later in future years—becomes reality! It's okay to dream. God wants us to. It's exciting, a lot of drama, and fun!

The show *Star Trek* back in the 1960s had a big screen TV and cellphones. It had special instruments to detect energy or lifeforms, and ones with healing capabilities with lights and sound vibrations, and special natural herbs of course. All of these things we now have! Back in the 1960s, everyone would say that would be cool to have those things, but we all laughed and had a good time watching the show.

God wants you to know certain countries on Earth now have their own UFO's. We copied them from alien craft which crashed over the years since the 1950's all over the world. SO when UFO's are reported worldly, some are ours and some are from other planets. Yes this is 100% true.

Almost all of Hollywood movies we can in real life replicate. Any scene, any idea in real life some will be coming to reality in the near future. Don't laugh the new inventions are here and more are coming! Just like in the movie Avatar. We see all of the glow in the dark jungle plants. Do you know that we have them around the world now? Under the oceans we have glow in the dark creatures, flowers, and corals.

In deserts around the world we having glowing plants, cactus flowers. In the remote jungles of Indonesia, the Brazilian rain forest, Africa and Asia.

So here we have God's knowledge directly from him/her or from his/her Army of good, and aliens in the universe giving it to us! Get it...

God infuses our scientists' brains with ideas and inventions all the time, but says when we can have it or are able to handle it. Some aliens give us the ideas and the product itself, behind the scenes the hush-hush way, but they are physically presenting a product to our governments around the world.

God plays a little game with us sometimes and it is sometimes amusing. He will infuse an idea to about one dozen to one hundred people around the world, depending on how big of an impact of a product it is, or cure, or military weapon. Whoever acts on the idea first, and how they go about getting it ready for the people of the world and also who they know helps propel that idea. But all of the other people who didn't get the idea out first will lose, although some will not because they might have an offshoot of an idea with the same product.

People and Their Beliefs

I'm going to use my family for an example:

My *Father* – John J. Calabro, WWII vet, Marines, Japan Theater. Somewhat psychic but didn't totally dismiss strange occurrences. Believed there is more to it, but was very real.

My *Mother* – Happy-go-lucky type, just believes in God and old school church.

John (brother) – Oldest, believes in the supernatural and modern spirits somewhat. Old school Bible. Likes to talk about it.

Steve (brother) – Just old school beliefs. Doesn't like to talk about it at all. Not an advanced soul.

Joe (youngest brother) – Slightly advanced in spirit, but not totally. Always about the dollar and modern conveniences.

Gina (sister) – Good heart, but very confused and sometimes lost when it comes to God and spirits, but at least she's trying to believe.

My wife, Irene – In the beginning, she thought I was crazy, but now believes 100% what I know. Sometimes blows it off and doesn't like to talk about it, but she has gone to bed with me every night for 33 years. I would say she knows me pretty well!

She saw my body jerk in 2006 when the walk-in spirit actually entered my body. At 2 a.m., she saw me get flung to the floor from my bed in an astral travel battle with an evil troll, but I won with God's Army.

Dave (son) – Highly intelligent, 29 years old, graduate from a local high-ranked university. A high advanced spirit.

Sabrina (daughter) – 24 years old, believes all my adventures; when I tell her about them, she just says, oh well. True believer, but doesn't say much about it.

Brandon (son) – 22 years old, believes me totally, Manager of Corporate Accounts at a local storage facility. Here is somebody that is the accountant type. Quiet, to the point, and wishes me the best, totally believes everything.

My family who I live with are all highly intelligent futuristic souls that totally know what I know is 100% correct. I prove it to them just about every day.

Example: My daughter needed to pass her license exam for nursing, which she had attempted a few times. So I asked God time and time again, "What can I do for her to pass the test? It's very hard, even as smart as she is." So God told me one day, and as always I get the chills of confirmation or they make me see 33 or 333 or 1:11 or 11:11 on clocks or other places to confirm! They're not lottery numbers, trust me!

God said Sabrina needs to take another smaller course, but at a different location and when she takes the test, pick a far-away location like Plymouth Meeting. The time must be 12:00, not 12:30 or 1:00. A few days later, actually five days, she asks me, "Daddy, should I take this course at the University of Penn and Children's Hospital?"

I said, "Yes! Yes! Yes! Yes!" So she did and it was unique because the students came from the whole area from other universities together at one location.

She passed that and she felt great! A couple of weeks later, she said, "Daddy, I'm taking my test again, but it's confusing. Can you help me find a location and time?" She named about eight locations and three times: 12:00 p.m., 12:30 p.m., and 1:00 p.m. Can you guess what location and time she passed her test? Exactly what God told me. Yes, correct. Plymouth Meeting at 12:00pm.

GOD is right every time!
THANK you!

Investigator

By trade, I am an investigator, so by working with doctors and lawyers I learn a lot. Number one, they are both stubborn and snobby, not real people or common average folk. When I went to doctors' offices, I wanted to get in and out as fast as I could for fear I might catch some disease. When I was at lawyers' offices my work most of the times was not good enough, just to "break 'em" for me.

So one day doctors and lawyers wanted me to be at three locations at one time, so I said I'd had enough of the corporate world. I pulled over on the side of the highway and prayed to God. God if there is a way I can stay at home, collect a check and take care of my family, I want to do it.

God works miracles, again he proved it. That's what I've been doing every day since, but I didn't know he had a bigger plan for me. Being an investigator, I don't believe in anything unless I question the situation time and time again until I'm convinced and satisfied! Plain and simple, right?

I'm a skeptic and my own worst critic. Something has to be proved to me time and time again until God, my angels, and my spirit guides practically hit me over the head with whatever they're trying to tell me. That's why I wait too long to come out with the information!

Just like when I went to see this psychic. She said many things, but one thing stood out. "Dave, when are you writing the book, they ask me?"

I went to a guy psychic another time and he said the same thing. "Dave, they're telling me you are going to write a book." I denied it and blew it off.

The third psychic said, "Dave, when are you going to write this book!"

I said, "I don't have time, it's too consuming and stressful." I still didn't start until I listened to George Noory's guest on angels on the *Coast to Coast* radio show.

When she said, "George, I almost didn't write this book. I'm glad I did. I would have regretted it." At that moment, I said, "I will write the book, then." Then chills and pulsations rushed in my head to confirm it, followed by the warmth of confidence from God!

My Father Died In 2003

When my dad died, I wanted to know why he died at this time. Why did he die of asbestosis and diabetes from the doctor cutting him up too many times to get the asbestosis out? It was a lose-lose situation.

When I saw him the last time, sitting up in a hospital bed at Taylor Hospital in Ridley Park, the family was there, asking many questions. But one thing stood out to me and I'll never forget it. He didn't even look at anybody there and he said, "Whatever the good Lord wants to do, it's up to him."

That there said it all, and that was the cue my dad was checking out. I call it getting beamed up. Beam me up! And that's the way it is, very similar, as I explain later in the book. My dad didn't have a chance.

As an investigator, these are the major questions. And here is the answer straight from God (the creator for Atheists). Atheists crack me up by the way and are funny. They just don't know, so they look for the easy way out to analyze life itself.

When all of us are up in Heaven, we are made of God's light. That's why the Bible says that we are made in God's image, meaning you soul is God's energy light, a special essence formula, if you will. Up there nobody or nothing can hurt you or destroy you. We are all feeling like Superman and Superwoman up there. When we want to come to a planet for a physical lifetime, we write out our story and record it up there. Even why we die, how we die, when we died, and of what way or disease!

We know we're coming back to heaven when we're writing our story.

Drama

Human beings are all about drama. It's our nature. Whether it's sports drama, mob drama, love drama, losing someone drama, comedy drama. We love any drama. When my wife is watching shows on the "women's" TV channel, she always wants to see about a girl being murdered and crying out loud. D.R.A.M.A.

When a mob movie is played and a guy slices somebody's neck and chops up the body. D.R.A.M.A.

I said to my wife, "why are you watching that stuff?"

To which she responds, "It's interesting." D.R.A.M.A.

On Earth, we are all players on a stage and you are the main character. You don't have to be in Hollywood or New York to be an actor. You already are. This is confirmed 100% true and correct.

When my father died, I needed to see a social worker because I lost my best friend. Remember, we went everywhere together and I was his black sheep of the family. I went see a woman named Amy, a social worker around my age. She is the best! She's the only one that would fully listen to me and I had her full attention! I know it's her job, but I didn't care. My words and experiences had to get out. I was climbing the walls, not telling anybody but my family. She also has the best advice.

I also saw Amy because of my fall on the ice on two different occasions. I fractured my L4 and L5 in my back and fractured both hips! A slip on ice is understandable for back damage, but not for BOTH hips. Something strange was happening.

No Operation

Healing bones on your own is hard enough, but doing it without an operation is a true 100% miracle. No question. During my four-year total healing process, I have seen or had contact with:

1. Twelve psychics
2. Five Reiki healers
3. John of God from Brazil
4. Three Physical therapists who didn't help much
5. Past Regression Therapists
6. Shamans healing me in other dimensions

I also prayed day and night, tried to walk on my own, and did certain exercises.

In total, I am 90% healed in both hips and not 100% yet because God still wants me to learn. I was told the reason why I had fractured hips at this time in my life is that I wrote it before I came to Earth; it's to make me more spiritual for my soul to progress! Bingo!

Strange Things

Strange things started happening to me. I would walk my dog, Reggie, a mini Doberman, and all people would come up to me. They would talk about Reggie, but then they would switch to asking questions about me! I named the dog after Reggie White, the famous Philadelphia Eagles' pass rusher. He was one of the great ones, but you might say people come up and say hello to dogs all the time...

Anyway, a tall beautiful woman came up to me to say hi to me and the dog.

"What a handsome dog," she said, but then she asked me questions. "Do you live around here? Where do you work? What's your future life? Are you staying healthy?"

I said, "What!? I just met you, honey."

She was gorgeous and tall. I asked her a few questions, like "what's your name?"

She just wouldn't tell me and started to ask me another question.

Then I asked her, "Where are you going?"

To which she replied, "To work." Then, with a smile, she started to walk away.

I asked where she lived and she said she lived around the corner.

For the next month, I walked Reggie that same way day and night at the same time and I never saw her again. She was perfectly beautiful and her eyes were strange, not only their shape, but they also changed color. I thought I was seeing things.

Another time I bumped into an old man and he asked for a dollar so I gave him one. He was a nice old man, but so squeaky clean, he couldn't live on the street. He had a special twinkle in his eyes.

He started asking me questions like the beautiful woman. Are you staying healthy? Are you working? What an unusual dog I had. He said, "That's a special dog. A keeper."

Anyway, I said, "I have to go."

He asked if I needed money.

I said, "What?" An old man asking me for a dollar and then after the conversation asked if I needed money.

He said, "How much?"

I was stunned.

Then he said, "Here's ten dollars, take it. Then when I see you again, you pay me back. Then I will give you more money."

I walked my dog every day the same route and never saw that old man again!

Another time four kids—three boys and a girl, all in their young teens—were laughing and throwing peanuts at me while walking the dog.

They said, "Can I have your dog, mister? He's nice."

I said, "No, get out of here."

They continued to follow me but were playing around with me by each one of them tugging and hitting my jacket and pants! I had never seen these kids before and I've lived here 22 years. I'm an old football player, broad shouldered, and not timid looking. Nobody ever messed around with me.

Either these kids were goofy or they were from out of town. But they were constantly laughing and fooling around. I said, "Where's your parents at? Where do you live?"

They said, "We don't have any mom or dad." They laughed. Then they said, "We live right there." They pointed to a rundown row home where I thought nobody lived. They finally left and stopped bothering me.

I was confused. Shocked! Nobody ever did that to me my whole life. So I followed them, me and Reggie. They sensed I was following them so they ran around the block and me and Reggie ran too. As soon as I turned the corner they were gone! Nowhere in sight. I looked around with the dog that whole city block and never found those kids.

Every day and night I looked for those four kids, never to see them again, very strange.

Indian Powwows

I found a powwow on the computer and just went to one with my wife and kids. By this time my wife and kids know what I'm all about. These powwows were fascinating, with all the native outfits and native sons and changes, native jewelry, and even handmade weapons!

An Indian girl was giving out papers so I read one. It had on it a reading by Silverhand, a great seer (psychic) from many generations. I went to meet with him and his wife and had a reading. He told me a lot of events and gave me wisdom. I told him about my astral travels and I wanted to know what they meant. Here it goes...

He said, "You lived many lifetimes. You are an old soul and have a lot of knowledge, but you still need to get much more knowledge from spirits for your future journey."

He continued, "You were part of the Nez Perce tribe out west at one time in the 1800s in Idaho/Montana and Washington/Oregon states. You were a great warrior, almost next in line for a chief, but you were shot in the head and struck by an arrow in the chest by another tribe." He told me that I used to train and take care of the spotted appaloosa horses.

I've had a couple more readings from him and he was right on the money. He is like my father in some ways: a good soul, a leader, a lot of wisdom. Thank you, Silverhand.

I saw many psychics and they're correct 85-90% of the time. Their visions come at all different times in your life. Sometimes through the veil, where they get their information from Spirits, words and quotes sound alike, but have different meaning. The spirits have high-pitched sounds and the info might sound like something else, or the psychic is under the weather and vibes are thrown off!

Native Americans

I have much respect for Native Americans. They have a tremendous amount of wisdom and demand respect. I am always seeing Native Americans in my astral travels. They are always healing me for something whether it is my heart, legs, liver, your souls energy or your worried mind. I go out back in my yard at night and look at the stars. I light up a native white sage and send my prayers and thoughts to the heavens. Try it sometime, it is very relaxing.

I've encountered three native women older to younger, a shaman healer, a gathering of tribes and my number one spirit guide besides my astral double, whose name is Chief Red Hawk. He is a stunning silvery white sparkling diamonds figure that looks about seventy something year old with a beautiful chief headdress that flows all the way down his back to the ground.

His facial features are wrinkly and a stern look that means business. This is one chief you do not want to mess with, not even to joke around a little bit. There are consequences and he will let you know it. God wants you to know to study the ways of Native Americans because they are wise and very patient.

When they sit at night whether around the campfire or inside their tee-pee they are always teaching and learning. The way that they do it is learn everything along with spiritual meaning behind each learning project no matter what the subject is. I wish that Americans today can be more spiritual or I say universally spiritual. Meaning the whole Earth and the Universe. If everyone in America was spiritual the world would be a much better place.

What God wants you to know is other countries around the world are raised to be spiritual first. That's the way it was when we were first on this Earth. God wants you to recognize him then everything else falls into place.

God wants you to know that patience is the number one thing to learn because it is combined with everything you do here on Earth. Do you know why? It is because "patience brings perfect timing". That is for everything you do! This is why God wants you to know. That He, your angels, and spirit guides (friends) on the other side, and your astral double all know your whole life ahead of you! Yes this is confirmed 100%. This is also how a good psychic communicates with the realms.

The Meaning of Life in A Nutshell

They all tell the psychic what you need to know. The things you want to know come at different times in your life so this is where the patience comes in. You can't hurry up your life like that. That's just not the way it goes up there.

For Example…

If you want to get married this year, and you say it is a must for this year the psychic may tell you five to six years from now. But you want to hurry it and it will be a mistake. Your guides know it is not the right time for you now, and it might not be the right person! But you will say this, "Oh that psychic doesn't know what they're talking about! She or he is a fake!" No they're not fake, they are only telling you what your guides are telling them because they already know your whole life story. Get it? Your guides have the perfect timing for you.

God wants you to know…did you ever work on something, any project especially of your great knowledge and expertise and it hardly ever works out for you? Think about this. No matter how much knowledge you have or how hard you try or even sneaky or multiple ways or every possible direction it just doesn't happen. That is because it is in no way the perfect time for you to do that project. It might be another day, week, month, or year for that matter. So God wants you to know again you need perfect timing for that to happen! Okay!

This is why Native Americans and other countries around the world are more spiritual. We Americans teach the world to hurry up and make the money but that can lead to a stressful unhappy life. A small to medium business is fine but when you are told to expand the business it always turns into stress and more troubles! You should always keep a steady pace. Don't stress to get more sales. Let it come to you. If that's all the Universe is giving you then be happy!

If you're going to expand the company just hire one or two people to do your work and you just relax and do your favorite things. Just live a slowed down modest life with hardly any worries is best. Just go around helping people a little bit! When you help anyone too much it will start to stress you out and you will mess up that persons life with too much help and make them lead into another direction so moderate help, okay?

With a regular job you don't always have to strive for the biggest position. Head manager, vice president or CEO. If you are comfortable where you are in the company that is where you belong. Do not deceit or make wrong doings to climb the ladder. If it was meant for you to climb the ladder in the company they will notice you and pick you! Why stress over it? Remember stress is the number one killer.

God wants you to know that like many tribes there is a perfect place for you, a perfect role to play, and if that time comes for you to move on so be it.

Walk-In Spirit

In 2006, I was walking from the kitchen to the living room and my wife was laying on the sofa. When I was at the dining room, about to enter the living room, my body jerked in all different ways that it never had before. My hips went left, my shoulders went right, my head and neck went different ways, and my legs jumped! Wow! Yes, this is true.

My wife saw it and said, "Are you okay?"

I said, "I think so, what just happened?"

My wife wanted me to get checked out by the doctor. I was okay then, but in a few days I went to get checked out anyway.

I received a full exam and my doctor said, "David, nothing is wrong with you."

I explained what happened, but the doctor said, "You're fine."

I found out later, after research, that there is such a thing as a walk-in spirit or partial walk-in spirit. I am a partial. Spirits rarely come into human bodies to help and take over, but this is because your present soul is crying out for help that you can't take it anymore on Earth.

When a spirit takes over they are highly intelligent, demanding to a point, but not overly. A lot of times they have great advice and know things head of time. They are caring and empathetic (empath)

They are critical of people in power (politicians and head of companies) and want to correct them. Don't forget they are part of God's Army and want to do what's right for the good of the people! They are also healers in many ways and like to counsel all people to help them out in any way.

Oh, by the way, for those of you who don't know what an empath is, it's somebody who can feel the hurt and pain of another person. Therefore, you know their personality pretty much and can help them cure themselves physically and mentally, you feel every hurt they have and understand them.

Seeing My Father and Mother in Spirit

Thursday May 14th, 2015

Strange things happen in my house. TVs turn off and on, lights flicker, and objects get lost and appear in the strangest places. You would think there is something wrong with my wiring, but we had it checked out! All of these events were witnessed by my wife and kids, sometimes neighbors. Here come the chills again.

My mother and father come to me in spirit now and then. One time, actually several times, my mother came to me while sleeping and my radio came on and off around 3:30 a.m. At that time is when most spirits are in tune with you because of your sleep cycle patterns. Lying in bed, I felt my right foot being tapped. I thought it was my wife or kids, but nobody was there. Then it happened again and again! I thought, me being a skeptic investigator again, that it was my reflexes in my foot, but no. The fourth time, both of my feet were tapped!

I asked God and the angels and guides for the answer and I prayed. I have to admit I was a little scared, shocked, and happy. Then, as usual, chills in stereo were filling my head then shoulders, and so on. But not warmth. The warmth only happens right after chills when God or a healer shaman is present, as I found out later.

Anyway, it was my mother saying hello and joking around because they showed me her dressed as a clown like she used to when she was here. She would dress as a clown at parties for the kids or a friends kids and for the New Year's parade in Philadelphia ever year! My mother did this to me several times, but I didn't have the visions this time.

My dad came to me when I couldn't sleep again. This is always the case when I can't sleep, I always feel like something is going to happen. I know I'm about to go somewhere astrally, always between 2 and 5a.m. I start to come out of my body, sometimes vibrate, sometimes not. I guess, depending on where I'm going, fourth or fifth dimension. On occasion, I hear a whoosh of water or chimes or wind. It all depends on what they want me to experience!

When I'm in my softball-sized form and not a baseball size (I can tell the difference), I usually sway like a slow balloon, but always to the front of me where I'm laying down on my back. This time, for some odd reason, I swayed to the extreme right side of the ceiling of my bedroom. I always sleep on the left side of my bed. I started my way up to the ceiling and I felt a presence.

I could not see this spirit, but he started talking to me because I was going to the unusual right side of my bed, but this voice sounded familiar. I was moaning, "Nooo....noo...God help me."

"Okay," the voice said.

"Okay, Daddy."

"Everything is alright."

"Go back, Daddy" Hey! It was my dear old Dad.

Nobody talks like that but him. He was going to "to frighten me, one psychic said. I laid in bed scared and happy at the same time. My dad visited me. I said, "What took you so long?"

I found out later from another psychic that their time is different up there, and when they finally figured it out because of confusion, they died or as I call it, were beamed up.

Time goes by for us. It might be months until they get adjusted to it, then they have a welcome party with dead relatives and friends they used to know. They are so busy talking to friends and our relatives that more months have passed. Then they go back to doing what they used to before being born. Get it? Only on rare occasions does a dead one see you right away!

Community College

Another time my mother and father came to me when my daughter Sabrina was graduating college for nursing. The day before the celebration, my wife said to me, "Dave, I asked all of our friends and relatives to come to the graduation and mostly everyone said they could not make it. There were all kinds of excuses, but that's okay because there's a mystery and reason for everything according to our creator. And don't forget they know our whole lives many moves ahead of us."

Anyway, I said to my wife, "That's okay, less people to deal with. Ha!" That night we went to bed and, as usual, I couldn't sleep, tossing and turning. I even had a couple of beers, but that didn't help. I started to vibrate like a cellphone and I said, "Okay, where are you talking me now?"

I came down on an angle in their dimension and they showed me the entrance of the community college. I always dropped my daughter in front of the college, so I never saw this section of the community college.

They showed me my mother. She smiled and said, "Hi, Dave."

My father was with her, but not smiling. You know how those U.S. Marine types are.

They were both in a bedroom and to the left of me they showed my mother, lying in a coffin. The first thing that they wanted to tell me to understand is that they were dead, but still existing. Wow again!

Wait! Excuse me while I stabilize myself. Every once in a while I have to stop writing this book. When I counsel people, the spirits zap and drain my energy from me and I get tongue tied, weak, and off course because sometimes I give too much information to somebody when I counsel them or write in this book.

But I want the world to know my experiences because I found out this is part of my mission in life from God, and he told me so in many ways and at different times. Besides enjoying sports, my other mission in life was to raise a nice family and to counsel people, free of charge.

Okay I stabilized myself....

My mom proceeded to put her earrings on. You know, those old fashioned ones from the 70s. Turquoise in color, yes color! She also had a 70s dress or late 60s, you know, like in JFK's days.

Then my dad said to my mother, "Look at him. David looks like he's going to have a heart attack!" My dad was putting on his suit jacket and tie at the same time. When he said that, I was awestruck and anybody would be.

I wanted to say a lot. Had many questions, you know my investigations wanted to kick in, but I couldn't speak and it was only about 30 seconds. I looked to the right into the mirror and my face was white as a ghost and had a shocked expression.

Next, my guides and or angels—sometimes it's hard to tell them apart when you can't see them, but only feel their presence—they pulled me back into their hallway and said, "That's enough." They put me back in my body. But the last thing my dad said was, "This is how the good Lord wants it to be." And that's exactly how my Dad spoke. He would say, the good Lord!

How to Move in Space, the Fourth Dimension Way

One time out of body, I went right directly to space. I saw so many stars! I wasn't moving though. I was just staying in place, standing, but floating, if you will. Then somebody was talking and moving my arms and legs to show me that I could move certain ways in space. Left, right, straight up, down, on an angle.

It was like how astronauts move in space or in a deep swimming pool. That's all they showed me, so I went back in my body. Just another thing they wanted to show me I can do. Usually in the fourth dimension I'm flying over telephone poles down the street to somewhere. But it's definitely cool!

Fourth Dimension vs. Fifth

Every time I'm in the fourth dimension, I travel by floating through the air. Whether it's above street lights or moving in space, I can see that I am actually moving like Superman or a ghost. The fifth dimension is like *Star Trek*. You just get beamed wherever you're supposed to go and you're automatically there in a second! That's the difference!

When my mom died, all the girls went over mom's house to see her lying there dead. They were all talking. My wife Irene, my sister Gina, my sisters in-law Carol and Helene. When my wife came home, she said they were all standing around talking and all of a sudden they heard my mom breathing heavy like she used to during an asthma attack! Then the TV was going off and on by itself! They all ran out of the house!

My mother just wanted to prove to us that it was her because she's the only one with asthma like that. Case closed. Ok.

A World Reporter

I had to talk to other lightworkers here on earth about my experiences, so I left a message for the world reporter on phenomenon and strange happenings around the world. When Linda called me, I explained to her what happens to me like a lot of astral traveling. Like running into strangers and, after I talk to them, I never see them again, but they say they live around the corner or neighborhood. Like communication with angels and guides, and sometimes strong premonitions like hurricanes, tsunamis, and one I'm a little troubled by...the Earth getting slammed by Red Rock meteor/asteroid.

Tuesday, September 25th, 2012

I had this vision or astral projection that everyone in Philadelphia, and I assume on this planet, was being visited by other beings. I saw multicolored sparkled spheres in the sky at a distance and then they came closer fast! About half a mile to a mile up in the sky. People came out to look at them, but as they landed on the ground, some people ran to hide, and I was one of them.

Some stood there in shock and didn't know what to do, as if they were hypnotized. I hid under a desk in an office building, but they somehow found me fast! Why I was singled out, I don't know. Anyway, the beings picked me up with ease like they had some special powers with no effort.

They had human-like features. Tall, around seven feet, Caucasian, appearing all beautiful looking, handsome chiseled faces. No beards. Body thin, but not fragile like *E.T. the Extra-Terrestrial*. They wore silvery light blue, Spandex-type jump suits that looked molded to their bodied. They sparkled.

They put me on a stretcher and covered me with a white sheet. They moved me like I was on wheels, but I assure you I was not! There was the investigator coming out of me again. It's natural. I peeked from under the sheet and I was in a different place in another type of office or maybe one of their craft.

The next thing I knew, I was introduced to four beings. One was taller, a female with blonde hair like from the 60s and a foot taller, about 8 feet. I felt, by my natural senses, that they were trying to recruit me for some special mission. They gave me a light blue suit like theirs and as soon as I put it on it felt perfect for my body and I felt muscular, strong but not bulky. It was tight to my body, but not restricting. I felt youthful! They then proceeded to show me a device that was 2.5 to 3 feet long and 4 or 5 inches wide, a rectangular item. They started to tell me what it does.

- It's a naturalizer/multipurpose device.
- It is a stun gun or eliminator, but not like our stun guns; way better.
- It is a cloaking or disappearance device.
- It is a levitation device.

Two of the male beings, 7 feet tall with brownish hair and blond highlights or streaks, took me to a high bridge. The two beings just leaped over the railing and fell down.

But when I looked down about 40 or 60 feet, they were in the air and floating down, standing up, of course. Then they landed softly on the ground below, on their feet.

The woman told me to push the button on the device and jump down off the bridge, but I said, "No way. I can't do that!" They were training me for some kind of event. That's when I woke up. I guess I failed my lesson or I was not ready just yet. Since that time, I've had psychic readings from top psychics from all over the world.

I've had numerous tests. I told the reporter about being a star child partial walk-in spirit and was graded 31 out of 35 questions, 92 out of 100, and 53 out of 60, so that convinced me.

All psychics were very helpful, but the subject of astral traveling was very interesting. The book *Astral Traveling* said exactly what I've been experiencing, on the money! Now, since I can do this just about every night, I don't call for it to happen. What I do is let my guides and angels tell me to do, when they think I need it for a lesson of some sort, or to give me information that I should be learning.

When I travel, I was told most people are about baseball size or smaller. But I received information that I am a large softball-sized orb because I'm an older ancient soul with more experience with wisdom, and am open minded and fair to all beings.

You do sway like a balloon until you get to the ceiling of your bedroom or house, then you go through the ceiling or wall because you are God's light in his image, a Superman or Superwoman. I told Linda how I go through the stars and travel the speed of light and arrive at various places and planets.

One time, I was at a distance in space and I saw a planet and I was homing in closer to this planet I saw these dragon-like creatures who were showing teeth and making noise. There were many, a whole planet full. I was afraid, but my guides made me get very close and land on this planet. I was panicking, but they didn't do anything to me. They were friendly. I felt they were on my side. All they did was flap their wings and make soft noises now that I was with them. Before, as I was coming, they were loud!

I left feeling welcomed and loved so my guides wanted to show me that for a reason. They also showed me a planet with all different gemstones on it and nobody was around on this planet. I guess my guides wanted me to be happy and showed me the biggest cuts of diamonds, emeralds, rubies and more. Wow!

I was shown one of my spirit guides. His name is Red Hawk. He is a sparkling essence of energy with a chief headdress reaching the ground, all down his back. Very electrifying!

I also told Linda that I received a healing from an Indian shaman. I was healed mind and body, especially my physical heart, by three Native American women! One old, one middle aged, and one younger.

Another travel was how to maneuver in space astrally. They wanted to show me my family up there and I saw the light. First it was a pinpoint size and as I got closer it was way bigger, with four silhouettes of my family up there. Human shapes.

I told Linda that a good amount of times when the angels and my guides try to speak to me it's not like we speak here on Earth. They can't get through to me because I can't hear them through the veil on Earth.

So the best way they figured out was to give me the chills and warmth of love after that (if needed) to confirm to me that yes, I'm on course on what I'm thinking or saying is true and correct! Also, when another person says something that might be true and correct, they give me the chills. Sometimes nothing can be said at all between me and that person just standing next to them at a supermarket.

Another vision I told Linda about was a combination of a tsunami and a nuclear blast! It was coming off the coast, but I'm not sure if it was the east coast of the United States or some other coast in the world. There was hot air blowing—you know when you see heat coming from a hot asphalt road in the hottest summers—and tumbleweeds or brush trees bending. Then a huge wall of water, about 100 to 300 feet high. Fires started everywhere before the waves crashed!

The next thing I knew, I was out in space on a spacecraft; not far, a further distance from our moon. I looked out of the windows of the craft and saw a meteor coming from the right side of Earth and crashing into Earth, which splattered the color red up into space! I was told everything will be okay, but to what extent are they saying! Then I woke up.

Past Lives

Before this lifetime, I was part of the French resistance (not in the French army) I drove a sidecar with my girlfriend, One day, it was raining heavily in France and the Germans started bombing unmercifully. I fell in a military trench, and with all of the mud sliding and bombs hitting, I smothered and died under the mud. And to this day that's why I have claustrophobia.

Before that lifetime, in the 1800s I was in the Nez Perce Indian tribe in Idaho/Montana area. I took care of the Appaloosa horses and trained them. It was the time when Chief Joe was our chief, but before the cavalry attacked us. We had a feud with a neighboring tribe and I was shot in the right side of my head and struck with an arrow in the middle of my chest and died. I had total recall of the shot in the head. The other tribe also had guns besides bows.

Before that lifetime, I was an officer in the Roman Legion. Several times I gave the slaves and gladiators extra food and water. Other officers told higher up ranks this, and so they made me kneel and put a sword in my back and executed me!

For the longest time, about seven or eight years, I could never get the pain out under my left shoulder blade until I saw a Reiki healer and past regressionist in Philadelphia. She removed the pain by lightly touching my back and down my arm, through my left hand and fingertips. Wow. I cried. It was a moving experience and I thanked her. Wow! She said the pain under my shoulder blade was from the sword in that lifetime.

The oldest lifetime was in Egypt, when I was next in line for pharaoh and was killed by a close, jealous, so-called friend.

Healing On My Own

Two fractured hips is no joke! You can't put a cast on it, you're a cripple, and it hurts like hell. But when five doctors from a well-known institute want to slice and dice you for an operation and put something foreign in you like metal and plastic, well that was out for me. I told them all I was going to heal on my own with God and my angels! My wife and kids all though I was crazy, but I did some studies and healing and ate all natural. I did some exercises, and prayed day and night, constantly. But each time I spoke with a psychic, saw a Reiki healer, astral traveled to other dimensions, I was healing a little at a time. It took over four years, but there was a reason. My angels and guides wanted me to become more spiritual.

I suffered and healed up slowly because God wanted me to learn to be spiritual the right way for my special mission in life for him: to spread modern day spiritualism throughout the world through this book, to teach us what are truly his teachings and the meaning of life!

The Reiki Healers

They all healed me in some way, but they try to heal the whole body. They did the ancient bowl chimes one time. My left leg was hurting then. Now, I never get chills in my legs, but I was in some kind of a trance and the Reiki healer was saying, "Dave, you are asking, where are your friends in the other dimensions? They're saying they are here with you."

I said ask them, "Why did it take so long for you to come to me?" They told her there were many lessons that I had to learn on my own first.

She said, "Dave, I don't believe this, but he's saying that he's St. Michael and St. Gabrielle is with him too! Followed by St. Germain who watches over you the most."

My left leg started to get the chills for the first time, and no other part of my body received the chills.

She told me, "They are healing your leg as much as they can at this time because there is a reason they cannot fully heal it at this time. God wants you to feel the hurt to think more spiritually and talk to the Angels." She said, "Dave, they are telling me you must feel the hurt and the pain so you may heal others and tell them your miracle healing and blessings."

Now I get it! The Reiki healer never saw or heard anything like this before. She said something big is coming, a world event. Huge! I didn't totally understand, but I had a feeling.

I just want to say that eight out of ten doctors are just greedy for the money, and that's why I don't trust them or if I can avoid them at all costs. I do. Sorry docs, you all are too greedy, money hungry.

Going Crazy

Every time when I feel life is sometimes hard on this planet, I get many signs that I am not alone and everything will be okay!

I see 333 on clocks and street signs; people will say these numbers. I see it everywhere, 11:11 1:11 3:33, etc. When I'm sleeping, I just wake up to it and I see it on my clock. This tells me that my angels and guides are with me and confirming that I am on the right track in life. Then, after I see the numbers, I get the chill feeling again or static electricity, followed by a warming feeling of love.

I don't always get the warm feeling part. I don't know why, but they know what I need. Sometimes the pulsating vibrating chills are short—a couple of seconds—and sometimes they are longer, depending on the importance of the message.

Yes, this is how they communicate up there when hearing them through dimensions is hard. Words and sentences sound the same! Then they get misinterpreted and you think they mean something else. Two words can sound the same, and two sentences can sound alike and you will get the wrong message. That's why they chose another form of communication to me.

Sleep Cycles

When I astral travel, it can be at any time, but it's better when your sleep cycles or REMs are perfectly in tune! You also have to exercise and eat and drink things naturally. I only drink Evian and Fiji water because they come from a volcano and high up in the Alps.

You reach your peak astral travel time usually between 3-5am. When you eat naturally—nuts, seeds, berries, Evian/Fiji water—it cleanses the body, which make your cells and DNA alert and healthy. Everyone should do this. That's why, in ancient times, they were all very spiritual and in tune with the stars, dimensions, and mythical creatures and beings. Today we are so out of that. When DNA is healthy and alert, it goes right to the master gland in our brains, which is called the pituitary gland.

This gland is very special. Not only does it regulate the whole body, but it is also the direct connection to astral traveling and God! I'll say all of the medical field and scientists don't even understand it fully. Why? The doctors just want to make the almighty dollar and since they're so-called doctors, they don't want to believe it's the connection with God and angels and other worlds. And researchers don't want to be the first to say it controls spirituality with God, your soul.

Scientists are always arguing with the Vatican and God's spirituality, but they're both right! They work hand-in-hand together. Science is God. God is science. This I know for sure 100% true. So why argue? It's all together as one! But for centuries they couldn't figure it out. I'm here to tell you it is TRUE!

The pituitary gland is the small, pea-sized part of your brain, the master gland that East Indians refer to as the third eye. All seeing, seeing all.

It is situated in your brain between your eyes, for every one of us! Think of it as a homing device to God and the stars, a different world of dimensions. Yes! When this gland is in tip-top form (healthy) you will be connected to all that is God. This gland sends an essence of your soul from God to go and search wherever you want to go in the universe. Yes, universe. I've done this many times.

Your master pituitary gland is God's soul, God's light, when healthy of course. That's how the ancients lived. It's so simple and easy to figure out. It's sooo common sense that scientists and researchers, medical people, just miss it! HAHAHAHA. When is the human race going to learn again the truth?

I've read so many books lately, here is a list.
- All psychic books
- Astral traveling
- Religion (all)
- Ghosts
- The Animal Kingdom, including sea creatures
- All insects
- Politics
- Military around the world
- Astronomy
- Plants around the world
- UFO's
- USO's
- Genders male female, both!
- Technology
- Health (All types of healing)
- Psychology (personalities of many different people on Earth)
- Geology

★If I forgot anything I probably did read it some time ago.

Politics

What's wrong with politics today? It is ruled by too many insane, egotistical, no heart maniacs. That's who. They're all about the money and they want to rule too many countries and are trying to rule the world! Just like the board game *Risk*!

Here's what's wrong and how it works. A foreign country's government wants a strong military, right. So you have to buy them or give them the best weapons and food to stay healthy. When you do this, it makes the common people want food and supplies and they can't get it. So they revolt. The problem is, we give them, the people, weapons to fight when we should just give food and supplies for basic needs. The people also should practice not to have too many children (overpopulation).

We should never invade any country just to take it over like a board game. When the United States does this, all the fat cats make more money and they call it business or progress. It is not! When we take over a country, people all over the world hate us!

God and the angels tell me that this is wrong. The United States should just leave those countries alone and let tribes have their little skirmishes. They have been doing it for centuries. We should leave them alone! It is to cut their own population and there aren't enough resources for the people.

The United States will never have a decent, good moral leader unless God's army comes down and rules! This will happen soon enough. It was said to me 100% it will happen within one year, but on God's terms. And you cannot beat God's Army. He has unlimited phyla of angels, spirit guides, shamans, and there's no limit on the God's good army of aliens from around the universe. Also, I'm told our dead loved ones will enter the picture to also convince us that God is real and the ruler of all. Only at this time will the Earth lay down their weapons.

Our Military

Yes, we are the best in the world, but countries hate us because we kill their people and take over their countries for the fat cat money makers and politicians. Money is fine, but too much money is evil! It will ruin many lives, physically and mentally. You're just supposed to have enough to be comfortable and a little extra, this is okay with God. But most CEOs, if they lose a lot of money, they will jump off a bridge and kill themselves. It's against God's law! You will be put in a not so good holding area up in the other dimensions until you learn and straighten out. You will feel others' pain that you did to them over and over again. Your mind will go insane until you say you're truly sorry to God and all of the people you hurt!

Don't forget you promised God, before you were born in this lifetime, to live your life the best way you know how and to not ever give up, even through the heartaches and the pains. Our poor guys come home from a war mentally disturbed. This should not be! So many families destroyed.

In the future, we're going to have more robots for the military so no lives and families will be hurt. No live soldiers on the ground! The aliens are already giving us spacecraft like theirs. When you see a UFO or USO, you just don't know it, but it might be ours, some of them! Yes this is 100% true right now.

<u>Example</u> of our military politics being all messed up: We're fighting <u>with</u> an enemy (Iran) in Iraq to kill ISIS and Syrians, and then we're fighting <u>against</u> Iran in Yemen. Wake up, people.

Races

Do you really think that all of those different people came from one theory? Evolution? You are wrong, but not totally. I will tell you what God told me. Yes, God and God's Army of good aliens did put early people on Earth and yes it was an experiment!

But they got creative and started transplanting races from other Earth-like planets throughout the universe, but mostly from the Milk Way and Andromeda galaxies. So they're 100% TRUE. The idea was to see how multi races in physical form can get along and for how long. Because, on other Earth-like planets, there is only one race of people, maybe two on some planets. So there. Another "meaning of life in a nutshell."

Case closed. There should be no arguing about this from anybody. Everything I'm telling you is 100% true from God and my angels and guides.

Genders

God also tells me that he or she is both male and female, so if we are made according to the Bible, each one of us is male and female. That is why we all have male and female hormones in us. Now it depends on how much male versus female hormones we have at any time during our lifetime!

Even all the creatures on Earth—insects included, fish, everything—change genders in their lifetime! Check it out and study how the animal kingdom is. Go on the computer or to the library or watch a documentary. You will see.

Look at transgenders. They can't help themselves. They were programmed to change and that's it! We are so critical on this subject that it is a sin. Gays and lesbians are tortured for what God made them. This is not right. God said we were all made this way, but not everyone will tell you who they really are.

All insects and animals get along and it doesn't matter if you have more male or female hormones at any stage in your life.

The Bible

The Bible says man should be with woman. Yes! If you want to create an army! This is where the Bible is misquoted or misinterpreted. So if a male wants to be with a male counterpart and the same with females, it's okay. Maybe you don't want to make a tribe or bring 20 babies into this world to war and you can't take care of them. God gives us this choice! Freedom of choice!

Now, if the male or female couple wants kids, they can adopt and marry. It's perfectly fine according to God! It is NOT a sin!

★ The Bible only means male must be with a female <u>only to have children</u>. That's it. Not that it is wrong not to. Get it!

Yes, I'm all about family and that's what God wants, a happy family, but either way it's okay. 100% TRUE and correct. Case closed, no more arguing.

Terrorists

Terrorists believe the United States is the evil empire. These people have had everything taken away from them, and have been made to starve for long periods of time. If you went without food for days and not much for weeks, you would have your back against the wall like a rat and would want to fight the whole world, wouldn't you?

When terrorists cry out to the world, they just want help! Food, clothes, shelter, just like anyone else. Instead, we bomb them and starve them when they have nobody else to turn to and they turn to God for help. That's all they're doing.

In their minds, they can only turn into terrorists because they're fighting for God and their lives! American people don't understand but it's our greedy governments fault! Now you see! Simple, isn't it? Leave those countries alone. Pay attention to the American people and give them jobs. Those tribes over there have always settled their own disputes.

I am neutral. I am not for the terrorists. I only see it through God's eyes. And I'm not for our greedy government, either. I am dedicated to God's army of angels, guides, shaman healers, dead relatives, souls, and obedient good aliens. Okay! And I am also with the light workers on this planet whose DNA is advanced for the future. I am on their side. The ones that understand, like me. God's Army!

Technology

Yes, our technology is the best. Some ideas we are getting from good and some not so good alien technology. If you want to make the environment better, that's fine. When you're inventing too many war-like weapons and getting greedy like controlling the weather, that's bad.

Our medical and dental technology is getting better, but as usual they won't release the best technologies because it doesn't make them enough money! Here comes the greed again...

Our drug companies get people hooked on the wrong drugs: drugs that make you fat, drugs that make your body shake, drugs that mess your mind up. And don't you just hate those drug symptom commercials. I wish they were eliminated. Back in the old days, all we had advertised was

Alka-Seltzer or Pepto and aspirin, which are the basics. I hate those symptoms commercials with a passion!!

Health

If you exercise and eat naturally, okay you can cheat a little with two slices of pizza and only eat a half of a steak sandwich on a Friday night. Here is God's answer.

1. Eat as naturally as possible. Yes, you must eat naturally!
2. Exercise, even if you don't break too much of a sweat. It is still beneficial. I lost 29 pounds just walking in the park, not running because I was healing both fractured hips!
3. Avoid doctors. Not even for a check-up, because they will think of something to do to you. Then your mind will stress out your healthy body. Get it? Got it!
4. Remember, all doctors are money hungry. If you get a good doctor, you are lucky! One that's not greedy

and really gives you his time, is from the heart, and is serious about taking care of you.
5. Get whole body massages three or four times a year! It works wonders for body and mind.
6. Prayers, prayers, prayers. God, your angels, shamans, priests, saints, and guides would all like to hear from you as much as you can! They love it! To show appreciation, a thank you is always in order.
7. I don't even go to church! You don't need to. It's only for marriages and death services from the church to perform long ago rituals. It's okay, but do you really want to sit in God's house with all of those hypocrites? Besides, what's wrong with your house? It's not good enough? Ha! I don't feel like getting dressed up anyway.
8. Use natural herbs. I do. Like our parents, grand mothers and great grandmothers did. It is from God's Earth what else do you need to know.

Well God wants you to know to be one with mother Earth and use natural herbs! Always use herbs in moderation. I use half of a teaspoon of organic approved ginger powder to put in my coffee or tea but I don't use it every day. Every other day is moderation ya see. Ginger is used for easy digestion. I also use 4 tablespoons of natural apple sauce and apple juice in small glasses. That is what you mother was told to give you when you were a baby too!

The Meaning of Life in A Nutshell

If you need energy you can take ginseng but remember in moderation not too much. A little goes a long way. But God wants you to know proper sleep is so important you just don't realize it. It goes along with natural eating and drinking, very simple! Don't forget Evian and Figi water is best. A half a glass of fine wine is good even God approves that. Thank you Jesus and the Apostles. And by the way I did ask God, my angels, and guides on that and boy did I get the chills, vibrations and pulsations on that to confirm yes! It is okay!

Mythical Creatures

Anything mythical or fantasy always comes true, they tell me. If we humans think it enough, God says that's what my children want for their entertainment. Yes 100% TRUE. It just takes time for God to put things in order and to think of any consequences for humans. It's your free will from God.

The list of creatures includes all that humans see. The creatures will let you see them run, fly, swim, or jump away very fast, yes they are fast! When we pursue them, we do it slowly to be cautious. By that time, they are gone down the road, lake, or sky. We try to track them and it takes a lot of time and surveillance. We even get footprints or hair samples, but where do you think they go! In a cave? No! God tells me these creatures, all of them, run or fly away to, where else, their home where they came from. Their other dimension. They are all dimensional creatures.

Get it. Got it. 100% TRUE!

They are all super intelligent from the other side. They would never run into a cave. That would be silly! Where else would any intelligent being run to? Home, on the other side where it's safe. The only way you catch one of these creatures is if God lets us have one. I don't think that will be anytime soon.

But wait, the rapture is coming within a year. Very soon, so we will be in the fourth dimension. I think God will have his creatures around, but they will be friendly. The same with Loch Ness, the Mothman, ancient birds, Bigfoot, etc...

There are some creatures that our scientists make underground in labs. That's a fact, so you may have seen them around too. Yes our mad scientists are always working on some genetics underground. Far underground, aliens and humans work together on genetics to make creatures for any experiment. What? I thought everybody knew this?

The Devil

There is no devil as we know it. It is all in our minds, what we were taught growing up. If you eliminate suicide, that is. You break your promise to God to live it out. So, when you go up, dead—Beam Me Up!—you get put into a holding area. This holding area is God's time out for us to reflect on what we did wrong. Now, by denying that you did wrong, you will stay there longer. Of course it's dirty and you can't do much there but think. The caretakers there are from various places in the universe, so they might look alien, different, like a devil, but they do not torture you like in the Bible.

Your own mind will torture you because of what you did wrong. It will play over and over again. You will feel the pain and will be sorry until you cry out to God.

The Meaning of Life in A Nutshell

God and his angels will come to see you now and then to teach you where you went wrong. If they see you have changed for the good and are sincere and true to God, they will release you to the dimension you're supposed to be in and you will be fine.

Death
(Not Really)

Any way you die on Earth, it's usually the same process, except if you commit suicide. I told you earlier what that's all about. After your long, storybook drama of your lifetime that you wrote before you came here and made a promise to God to live it out, you simple vibrate all over and change dimensions. Easy, right?

You are first dazed and confused, then you realize you feel no hurt or pain. You are then greeted by your spirit guides and angels to get familiar with them again. You always are surprised and relieved when you see them and know who they are. When they think you are ready, they take you to God where God honors you for a mission well done and you praise God for the lifetime you've just experienced for your soul to grow and for the wisdom that you needed to learn.

After that, you will review your life on a scanner. You will laugh and cry. You will cry happy tears and sad ones. This helps your soul to grow to a ripe old wise soul that will live many lifetimes. If you are so upset and can't look at your life on the scanner, your guides will bring you to a calming health rejuvenation building until you calm down and get adjusted to how you were.

When you think you're acclimated to your new surroundings, they will bring you to your home galaxy/planet/city and your special studies where you started. All the people and relatives you knew in the lifetime and all of the others you had will be there!

They will sometimes look younger and healthier, or just the way you remembered them. Dancing, music, drinks and games for everyone! GOD IS GREAT! This is 100% TRUE.

God and Drama

All good and loving, God is both male and female. God can appear to you like anybody or anything seen or unseen. God is proud of your mission in this lifetime, whether it is raising a family, whatever occupation, or even a negative bad guy. God is watching.

God does have negative energy, but it's hard for us humans to understand his many steps behind the negative energy he brings to make you better. We humans are all about drama. Yes! All kinds of drama. There's sports drama, wedding drama, watching TV drama, injury or disease drama, fighting drama. You get the point.

How would you ever really learn much if everything went perfectly smooth all the time in all your lifetimes? You learn a lot more from a little or a lot of negativity, depending on what each individual needs to progress their

God's soul (or creator for Atheists). You would not learn much if everything went perfect like in heaven, and that is why we come here to Earth! Simple.

God knows your whole life story drama ahead of time. Each move that you make, so don't even try to fool God. You just can't possibly do it. God can be funny at times too. Yes, he's part comedian.

Like when you swore you just put your keys on the table a short while ago and they're now in your bedroom. Or when you're trying to find your glasses and you look all around for them and they're right there in your pocket or on your head.

This part of drama is very hard to understand, but is 100% true, so here it goes! All of life on Earth is a stage and you are the main character! 100% true. All the wars, all the tortures and concentration camps, tsunamis, earthquakes, volcanoes, shootings, stabbings, every one of them is staged because those souls know that they and you want to learn from Earth's fleshly experiences.

Yes! This is correct. Those souls that die know that they are going back to heaven and their lives as God's light beings, and they love it. No hurt, no pain, no diseases. You get to go do what you want.

These happenings, in turn, help you to learn about feelings of the families that are left behind. But everybody should know is that you too should be there soon enough. Don't forget, we are Superman and Superwoman up there, but come here for the drama, and we are proud of our lifetimes here. So proud that we write another one again and again and again when we're up there! It makes our soul wiser. It's fun. We love drama. It's what makes us human!

When people change dimensions (die), they don't worry too much about you because they know you have your own angels and guides to look after you. Plus, you must learn on Earth about the feelings of other people. Hurt, pain, suffering, that's how you learn. They know you will be up there soon, as well.

Heaven

What I'm told from God, angels, and guides is this: You are still you up there, but with total wisdom and a strong calmness of certainty that you, knowing all, with God's kingdom and other friendly souls have the utmost confidence and freedom of choice of your life. You are totally free and can do anything you desire, without criticism, embarrassment, or any wrongdoings! No hurt, no pain, no diseases. You are a superhuman soul that nobody or nothing can destroy. You are made of a special light essence, a substance of God the creator that nothing, even in space, our universe can destroy. Light cannot be destroyed, especially God's light. It can only be moved from one place to another at times and that's all! You can do anything your mind wants to.

For instance, if you want to take a trip to the beach or Las Vegas. Yes, there's Vegas up there. You have a choice which way you want to go there and with who and how many people. Other souls are doing this right now as you read this. You can either take a Corvette to your destination or old antique car, a hovercraft, a boat, a train, or a space craft. Anything you want, or you can blink like *I Dream of Jeannie* or beam down like *Star Trek*! How's that for God's work and rewards for your dedication to God for your trip to Earth? This you promised God to live out.

This is just one example of what you can do. You can also be with a group of aliens at a Halloween party or just lay on your back on beautiful grassy lawns and look up at the sky. You can also be with every animal you desire and as many as you want. They won't bite you or harm you in any way. After all, they're in heaven too!

Dealing With People on Earth Each Day

The negativity you feel and see from a neighbor or relative or business associate can be diffused and changed! Maybe that person is having a bad day and we mark him as ignorant, a bad guy. This person at that time of negativity is probably ill or a family member of his is ill and he's worried and irritated! Or things just aren't going his way at the time. So we tell other neighbors or relatives and coworkers that the guy is this and that. He's no good, stay away from him. So everybody does this to the poor guy for the longest time. Besides, he looks like you know what. Why does he dress like that or smell like that?

Well, you are on stage for God, your angels, and guides and for yourself. What are you going to do? Leave him alone for the longest time? Weeks, months, years, or help him in some way? Your choice!

If this individual is having just a bad day, then the next day or two he probably will be okay, smiling and being a good neighbor or coworker. But if it's more than that and his mother is ill, try to console him with positive thoughts or look up on the computer for a remedy for his mother's ailment or facility for them. That would make you a better person and you will look good on stage (your life).

The guy probably looks bad because he is depressed about his mother and he probably doesn't smell too good because he's taking a medication that his doctor recommended. Now, if the guy gets helped out, here is how things can change by being positive to someone who is angry, doesn't look good, or has an odor.

Weeks later you find out that is mother's health is fine now because you made a suggestion for a new medical facility she went to. He feels better because you told him to ask his doctor to change his medication; now he has no odor, so he feels a lot better. He went to a couple of men's stores to pick out new clothes! Now he's feeling great and is a new man thanks to you for understanding. You receive an "A" for on-stage performance of your life, and receive merit points for good deeds with God or, for Atheists, the creator.

Variations of Vibrations

-A spirit guide is ... small to medium vibrations, usually just in my head

-An angel is ... medium to large vibrations changing to pulsations.

-All three ... God, angels and guides. Pulsations are stronger than vibrations.

here is nothing small to medium. All vibrations are t¹t to large pulsations that run all throughout my o⁵ody down to my toes! This is followed by a loving ʰat's incredible, a super calm, strong, positive, in therᵢfidence.

By the way, they also communicate by 33 3:33 1:11 11:11 11:33. Seeing these numbers are no not for the lottery like most people think, me included at first. I found out that these are spiritual numbers to confirm what I were thinking at that moment or if someone just said something to me. This happens to me all the time and is 100% effective and correct!

Just a note, when I counsel someone or talk about spiritualism, I get drained of my energy so much that sometimes I forget to eat or drink something. The information I need to tell somebody is draining on me because a lot of information needs to be told to that person. Including the writing of this book!

I lose track of time because I kind of get put into a trance. I sit by my koi fish pond alone to clear my mind because of all the strong energies. So if I do this, and eat and drink naturally, I regenerate my mind and body.

All religions around the world believe in an intelligent higher power. This is very good, but their customs and walls leave other people out for all reasons, such as:

- They are a different race
- My race is better than theirs
- You do not look like me
- You do not dress like me
- You do not speak like me

Inspirations and Motivations

- God
- My angels
- My spirit guides
- Shamans
- Reiki sessions
- Amy (counselor)
- All the people I counseled, young and old
- My pets, dogs, cats, turtles, fish, birds, etc.
- Local and world psychics
- All religions
- St. Mathews church
- All of Nature
- Science
- UFOs and USOs

- Pastors around the world
- World history and news
- Comedy
- Philadelphia Eagles football
- The city of Philadelphia and suburbs
- My friends and family in the spirit world
- All my people in my neighborhood in "South Philly"
- My kids David, Sabrina, and Brandon
- My wife Irene

Thank You

To my buddy Skip,
   Thanks for getting me to parties to relax and getting my mind off of these strange happenings for a while! I needed it.

To my wife Irene,
   Thank you for sticking by me through all the crazy and hard times. Now you believe me. All the strange things that happened in our bedroom, with all the spirits and astral traveling, especially the negative troll energy spirit that knocked me off the bed, but I still won, beating that bad energy.

To all of the people I meet each day that I counsel in healing and advice, thank you. At the bars, all of South

Philly, down the lakes, Murph and crew, all of the people hanging out on Broad Street, Snyder Ave, the shopping malls. Thank you for admitting to your strange phenomena. I helped you guys and you helped me learn and confirm what I was experiencing and you all were afraid to tell anybody for fear you were ridiculed and laughed at!

I want to express a NO thanks to the millionaires I asked to donate to the making of this book. You are all too greedy. Shame on you all for not donating some funds for the making of this book! You cheap S.O.B.'s. I did it all on my own!

I heard all of the excuses. Please do not look up to rich people. Look up to God and his army.

God Bless Everyone.

Closing

To the people of the world, our DNA is changing for the future and for the good. Be ready for the big change. It will be great for all. It will be the biggest show on Earth, the most drama that human beings crave! Very exciting. All emotions wrapped up in one.

Be good to your relatives, neighbors, and friends, because you don't know their pain, illnesses, and hardships. Always help with positive energy. We have enough negative in the world.

This information must be presented to the world so people will understand what true universal spiritualism is! Talk to and be dedicated and open-minded to your God, angels, and guides, because everybody on this Earth has them.

Ever since 2006, when I became a walk-in spirit star child, when my body jerked in all different ways just walking from the kitchen to the living room, my wife witnessed this and said, "You are not yourself. You are a different person." My three kids agree! But half of my higher dimension self walked in me and I'm glad. I'm smarter and have a better understanding for everything

Since then, God, the angels, and guides tried to speak to me by sound. They used regular sentences, but this information was not getting through for some reason. All I heard was mumbling and some words, very little; not enough to figure out what they were saying to me. I could however tell if they were male or female spirits. As time went on, they created a new method of communication to me. Vibrations! Sometimes it's a small amount or a lot, and sometimes it's in between.

This is how it goes when I am speaking to someone or they are telling me something or I only have to be near that person from a distance. A lot of times no words are exchanged at all. I start to get a vibration in my left side of my brain, then the right side starts, then they pulsate together in rhythm, like stereo.

The next thing that happens is the vibration energy static chills pulsate down my whole neck then my upper body, next to my lower body and legs and feet. Following that, starting in my brain again comes a calm but strong warmth of love that soothes me and lets me know that

God and the angels are confirming and saying yes to whatever I was thinking at that moment or what I said to an individual in counseling or what that person said to me! Now, it's all according to the topic and if it's important to me or to them.

Remember, they run the show. They control what information needs to be let out and at what time, day hour, week, month, and year! For instance, I would ask them, "Should I write this book?"

Their answers were always fast and strong pulsations with God's warmth afterwards, but if I ask if I am going to get a new car soon, they won't pulsate at all, even if I ask many different times over weeks! I found out that, when the time gets closer for a new car, they will pulsate a little, just enough. Remember, it's all according to importance to them! They control what's important to me and the human race.

Things to remember

1. You are the star in your lifetime. Think of it as you are in your own Hollywood movie. You are a fleshy projection of your higher self(Astral body). You are god-like(your soul) and part of Gods army of light. Even when you die you will never cease to exist.
2. Use natural herbs in small doses. Remember they have been used for centuries.
3. Patience with everything you do. Your rewards will come with perfect timing.
4. Know your comfort zone and your place in life.
5. Be comfortable and not greedy about money.
6. Any negative setback is a learning process. It is God's way for you to learn. It is not the devil. God will always make you better but you must learn the lesson

he gives you, out of the negative setback, he gives you, no matter how harsh it is.
7. Laugh a lot. Comedy is a very good remedy
8. Now! How great is God! Stop saying why did God do this to me. You wrote your own lifetime story.

David P Calabro

The Crystal Ball

The Meaning of Life in A Nutshell

Healer:
Old Native Woman blowing sage smoke on me for healing. All white long hair, about 75 years old.

Middle Age Indian girl, about 25 to 35 years old.

Young Indian Girl, about 18 to 20 years old.

Native Indian Woman Healing

David P Calabro

Chief RED Hawk
in Silvery Diamond
Sparkles

My Main Spirit Guide

The Meaning of Life in A Nutshell

Native Indian Shaman

David P Calabro

Seeing the Light and Four Human Figures

The Meaning of Life in A Nutshell

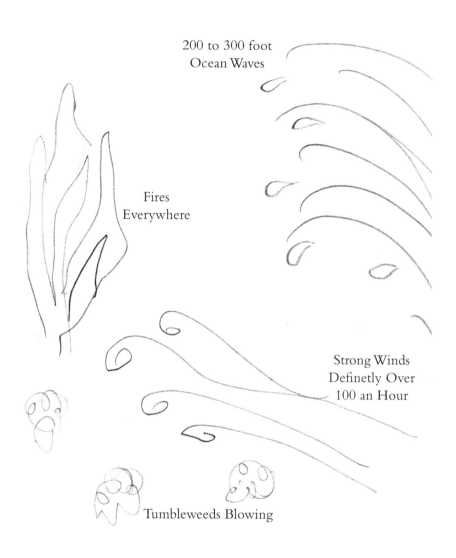

Something Huge Coming

Notes

The Meaning of Life in A Nutshell

Autograph

About The Author

David grew up a normal all-American kid and excelled in all sports, especially football. He had a happy well-rounded life. With three brothers and one sister, he was the middle sibling. Life was fun, exciting, and adventurous, with many barbecues, fishing trips, nightclubs, movies, and neighborhood drama! His dad was a WWII marine who had fought in Japan. The two of them went everywhere together. All of his uncles were also in WWII, but when his dad passed—that's when everything started to get really strange!

By trade David was an investigator, now retired, for all law firms and medical facilities in Philadelphia, PA, and from New York to Washington, DC. He is a huge skeptic because of my trade. He must check anything he deals with over and over again to make sure it is fact! When all of these out of body experiences happened, he had to make sure that they were real. When he saw his mom, dad, relatives, and pets on the other side … it was real.

David astral travels about every other night. He is now a partial walk-in spirit of his higher self. From the future, he is also an empath of people's feelings, as well as a healing counsellor for the mind and body. He is a lightworker of God's army, and one of the star people.

CPSIA information can be obtained
at www.ICGtesting.com
Printed in the USA
BVHW032115280319
544008BV00001B/3/P